COLLECTION OF SHORT STORIES

SUNIA BASU

Copyright © Sunia Basu
All Rights Reserved.

This book has been published with all efforts taken to make the material error-free after the consent of the author. However, the author and the publisher do not assume and hereby disclaim any liability to any party for any loss, damage, or disruption caused by errors or omissions, whether such errors or omissions result from negligence, accident, or any other cause.

While every effort has been made to avoid any mistake or omission, this publication is being sold on the condition and understanding that neither the author nor the publishers or printers would be liable in any manner to any person by reason of any mistake or omission in this publication or for any action taken or omitted to be taken or advice rendered or accepted on the basis of this work. For any defect in printing or binding the publishers will be liable only to replace the defective copy by another copy of this work then available.

Tattoo

Once upon a time, a lover boy. He made his girlfriend a tattoo on his back side shoulder. His name is Macho and his age is 21 years. His girlfriend's name is Mary. He loved her so much he could do anything for her. He heard a fast and furious game was going on. The winner gets rs- 5,00000 and the runner up gets rs- 2,50000. The game will start at midnight, at 12:00 AM, because it is an illegal car game and risky too. Macho took part in it because of the winning number. His girlfriend said to not take part in it because it was too risky. He said, do not worry, you are with me" na. She say what you mean to say? He said I means to say your tattoo with me, for that nobody can touch me. Then he says," now you understand?" She says yes. Now he has a tattoo on his right hand with his girlfriend's name. Macho takes a car. In that car, his girlfriend also had tattoos there. On the car seat belt his girlfriend's tattoo is there. The car inside and outside, everywhere his girlfriend's tattoo and name were there. The car race started at midnight at 12:00 AM. After some time, someone shouting, dying is dying. Please help me, but the race going on can't stop helping him out. He is trying to get help from road going people but they are also busy watching the race.
Then he again shouted for help. Nobody came forward to help him. In the meantime, the race comes to the final round. We are all very excited to see who will win the race. Macho's car is a lot away from others but he tries to come forward. He speeded up his car and came closer to the winner's post. Rocky is still in 1st place. Still now nobody crosses the rocky car. Suddenly, Macho crosses a rocky car and reaches the winner's post. Rocky finest as a runner up. Macho gets a winner's check and the trophy. Then he went back home and called his girlfriend. At that time, the 4:00 AM clock show. His girlfriend did not take his phone. He gets very angry and sleeps. Next morning, his

mom called him for breakfast. He says I will not take breakfast. His mom said," Why are you OK?" He said yes. He asked why she did not take my call? His mom said she was sleeping at that time. That why she can't take your call? He says it is OK. Then go for breakfast. I just went to his room and dressed my clothes and went out. Then he went to a tattoo shop and again had his girlfriend's tattoo on his left hand. Tattoo man say to him any more place is remain in your body for tattoo. He said no and went back home.

Then, his girlfriend mary call him at a coffee shop for coffee and then go to a movie. Macho tries to see her with his left hand tattoo. She said again and again, saying to go to the movie, but Macho in his own way. Macho belongs to a rich family, so he does not have problems. He made his whole boby with tattoos, not even leaving his private place also. Now Macho takes her to a tattoo shop to have tattoos on her hands, but she does not want to have tattoos on her hands because it is so painful. Macho forces her to have tattoos on her hands. She only allowed Macho's name in her hand. Then come back from there. She wants to kiss Macho, but seeing their also tattoo, she get angry and go back home. Macho has a tattoo mania but he love mary very much, so he makes his whole body a tattoo of his girlfriend. Mary thinks it is madness, not love. Then she also wanted to married Macho. Then they get married and live a happy life.

------------------------------- The End -------------------------------

Pooja Aur Micky

This story belongs to Pooja and Micky. Pooja lives in a small village with her grandfather. Pooja's grandfather is a brick maker. Pooja helps him with brick making after school. Her grandfather sent her for higher studies to a brick-maker's house. Pooja does not want to go there. Her grandfather took her and left their house. There Pooja meets Micky. Her father's name is Joydeep Kapur and her mom's name is Sima. Micky is their only son. Pooja comes to study and takes care of Micky. She can't speak English. She brought a rose tree with her from her home. She gives one rose every day to Micky. Joydeep gives her bicycle to go to school. His wife is an actress, so she say Pooja to carry make up Kit Box at school time. She did not allow her to go to school. She said after coming back from the shooting spot, just do home work like washing clothes, ironing clothes, wash room and take care of Micky. Pooja studies at night when everyone sleeps, so no one can know about her studies. Micky is a 5-year-old girl. She can't eat food alone.

Pooja gives her lesson by singing and playing. Before Pooja came, Micky failed in all subjects. Her class teacher says give her a private tutor and then you see the result will change. He just fooled his mom. Micky does not like him. She just made her face angry and said, just go from here, but her sir can't listen it. Micky enjoys Pooja's company. Pooja makes her happy every time. Now Micky comes first in class and the teacher says how is possible? Micky say is all for Pooja. If Micky shouts to Pooja, she can hear even though she is not there. One day Micky's school dancing competition will happen. Other students will dance. They said she would dance it better monkeys and dance. Pooja says you will dance. I will prepare you for it. Micky dances on the floor and all give a standing ovation. Micky's classmates got angry and bit her. She shouted to Pooja. She came and said, can all be good friends with Micky." They shake hands with Micky. Pooja thinks we shall also go to a big house like others. She painted a house made of bricks and saw it to Joydeep. He was happy seeing that painting. One day, he asked Pooja for that painting. Pooja shawed him. Pooja gave that painting to him.

He got the idea from that painting and he became a big builder. Now they shift to a new house with a garden. There they have different types of flower with roses. Micky loved Rose very much. They played on the terrace, by playing with a nail that was stuck on Pooja's leg. Micky's mom scolds Pooja and she says" You'd not see it if it stuck on Micky's leg. Then she said just go and have a bandage, then do the work. Pooja has so much pain in her leg that she can't do any work, but Micky Mom does not listen to anything. Next day, in the evening, she throw Pooja with her bag outside the house and she said to not come here again. Someone took her to the hospital because blood came out from her leg. That hospital head took her to bed and washed her leg. Then they bandaged her leg. After a few days, Pooja said" my leg is good now. I can go home now. The doctor says you have to take a rest a few days more. The doctor and her husband took her to his home as their daughter. They send Pooja to school where Pooja speaks English. Pooja learns English from Micky. She gave an exam and selected. One day, Micky comes to that hospital for treatment because her eyes get hurt and bloody coming out. Sister's are saying that her mom throws a fork on her eyes. Pooja listened to that and said to the doctor to give her eyes to Micky, but she did not know that she was a cancer patient. She could die anytime but she wanted to try to go to Micky's cabin but she fell down and she died. Pooja wants her eyes given to Micky. The doctor also gave Pooja's eyes to Micky, but Micky said if Pooja did not come then she would not open her eyes. The doctor says you just open your eyes slowly. Then she opened her eyes and searched for Pooja. Her dad says Pooja is in Rose now. Micky now plays with Rose every day.

-------------------------------- The End --------------------------------

Agreement

This story belongs to Bunty and Bunny. She lives in London and hates India. She has a clothes boutique and bought everything from

India. Bunty and Bunny's grandfather leaves properties for them which value is in crore rupees. They have 3 conditions and letters can be opened after when both are 18 years old. The story starts here now. Bunty is now 23 years old and Bunny is now 19 years old. Bunny flies to India to read that letter given by her grandfather. He gave it to his advocate and Bunty's grandfather also did the same. Here one thing is common, that both sides advocate is the same. The advocates give one letter to Bunty and give one letter to Bunny.

Bunty read the letter first and said it was impossible. His grandmother asked what happened? Why did you shout? He said," Here written you have to get married first, then you get the property. Now Bunny said here also written same. Bunty's grandmother says you first talk with each other, then you plan anything. They said it was impossible we did not know each other. How could we get married? The advocate said you have no other option. If you want property, you have to married and live with each other for 1 year happily. They said we needed some time for thinking.

After some days passed, they agreed to marry. Then an advocate gives a second letter. It says you have to stay in one room for 1 year. They agree with that also. Bunty does not want to work, only lying in bed all the time. His wife took a school job, then his ego hurt. Now he plans to go to the office and look after their business. His friends said give a party. He said why? His friends said," You got married, that's why we want a party. He said it was a 1-year marriage agreement only. You can say just a game. It is not a real one. He said," I just agree, for money, that is all. After some time, his wife passed away from there with someone sitting in the car. He felt angry and broke the beer bottle. You just said to us it is not real, then why do you get angry? Do you love her? His friends said, ask yourself first. Then they sent him home. At home, his wife said, are you jealous?" He said no, I am finding" cause of divorce. Bunny cried and said," You are a heartless person, but Bunty does not hear it because he sleeps. Next morning, when Bunny was ready to go for work, then bunty said," can I drop you? Bunny said OK. Bunty dropped her and went to the office. This way 1 years gone. Then advocates give a 3rd and final letter. Their have written that they have to be good parents first, then they get the properties.

They do not want a baby now, but for cause they think so. They celebrate their 1st anniversary on an air balloon. The anniversary cake was cut in their bungalow. Bunty's friends are invited and Bunny also.

They enjoy the party with music and dance. The next day, when Bunny is ready to go to school, Bunty said leave the job. Just plan for baby. Bunny said, what do you want baby now? Bunty said yes as say in final cause. Bunny said it was too early to do so. Bunty said if we are late and advocates will die, then we never get our property. Bunny said that was true. Bunny said we would talk in the evening. Now I am going late. Bunty also goes to the office. In the office, the advocate came and said you do not read full letter." Bunty said," Why? He said it was because your baby should come before your 2nd anniversary. Bunty said OK. I talked with my wife in the evening. In the evening, Bunty said to Bunny about full letter and said, what you do now? She said one option would be to remain. Bunty said, what's that? Plan for baby. Then, after a few months, they had a baby boy. Now they get their properties and live a happy life.

----------------------------------- The End

Chocolate

This story is chocolate love story. This story belongs to our school. Outside our school one chocolate shop was there. In school girl study in 10th standard and boy study in 11th standard. The girl name is Pinky and boy name is Vicky. The boy give chocolate to Pinky everyday. She taken as a friend. Vicky by give her chocolate he want proof how much he love her. Pinky do not understand that. She thinking is a friendship. When school over Vicky ask Pinky do you want ice cream? Pinky said yes but chocolate ice cream. Vicky said OK. Then Vicky take 2 ice cream and give one to Pinky. Then said can I drop you? Pinky said yes you can. Vicky give chocolate to Pinky again. Now she ask you give me chocolate every day like this? Vicky yes. Then Vicky said because I love you very much. She said really. Vicky said yes I means it. She said I also love you. Vicky hear it and so happy. He buy chocolate toy that made in chocolate and give it to Pinky. She love it. Next day Vicky pick up Pinky from home to go to school. Vicky have a car with driver. She ask you drop me home also like yesterday? Vicky Said yes I will drop you like yesterday. When they reach school, then in school gate Vicky give Pinky chocolate. Pinky take it and go to classroom. In tiffin time Pinky sreaching Vicky to take some chocolate again but she can't see Vicky there. She so upset that she not talk to any of her friends. After tiffin time over then Pinky have a game period. Her sir call all student to come. Vicky classroom it can clearly showen. Pinky sir play them bucketball. Nobody can hits to goal post. Then sir see them how to play bucketball? Vicky watch from classroom how Pinky are playing. Vicky teacher throw a chalk to Vicky to pay attention on lesson. He said to teacher what happen why to throw a chalk to me? His teacher said pay attention here not outside. Vicky now counting how much money he have to buy chocolate. After school over, then Vicky give Pinky chocolate again and said come to car. This way there life go on.

-------------------------------------- The End

Kangchenjunga

The Kangchenjunga Himal section of the Himalayas lies in India and encompasses 16 peaks over 7,000 m (23,000 ft). It is the third highest peak in the world. The most prominent peak in the Himalaya, after Mount Everest. It is also called K2 because it was the second peak in the Karakoram Range of the Himalayas to be measured. Kanchenjunga is shining like a diamond we saw in Gangtok in the morning from our hotel. The clear view coming is so beautiful I have no words to describe it. Everywhere we shone our torches it looked like a dead end. The whole of Sikkim feels like it is lying below you, glittering like diamonds. We heard from each other but now we see in front of our eyes. When the sun kisses Kangchenjunga peak it is also a wonderful view. We want to reach the Rishop for the best view of Kangchenjunga. Before we reached the Rishop, we stayed in Kalimpong for a few days. There we stayed in a tent and we were 5 couples who came here to enjoy the beauty of Kangchenjunga. It is too cold but we enjoy it with hot coffee. We can see the view of Kangchenjunga from the hotel balcony.

Next morning we started a journey to Kalimpong. In this cold weather, a love story began for my friend. He couldn't say her he loved her. The boys'names are Bunty, Vicky, Ricky, Raju and Rohit. The girls'names are Pinky, Rinky, Puja, Bunny and me Sunia. The love story begins with Raju and Puja. Raju tried to say to Puja that he love you. We reached Kalimpong tent where we had to spend a few days but the wind was blowing badly. What will happen? We do not know? Now we are going inside the tent. We force Raju to go to the puja in a tent and he goes to the Puja. She also did not say no to Raju. The mobile phones are also not working there. What other friends are doing me and Rohit do not understand. It was so cold that we couldn't drink water also. Next day we went out of tent and want to try mountain climbing. We try it and reach the top and then climb down. It takes 3 hours. Then we tried paragliding, flying and we did it.

We want to try a boat also, but the weather does not allow us. After a few days in Kalimpong, we enjoyed it a lot, but the weather does not support every time.

Next morning we started our journey to Rishop. Raju gets scared because he has problems at high peaks, but he still wants to go to Rishop. We said to him, do not look down, only see in front of you. Then we reached the Rishop the hotel and from the hotel balcony the best view of Kangchenjunga came, clear sky. Then we had our breakfast. Then we went for the side screen but everything was not up to mark, I think, because I missed the view of Kangchenjunga. Just sit on the balcony and see the view of Kangchenjunga. How time passes you will never know. In Rishop Kangchenjunga and Kanchenjunga shining like a diamond, we see from the Rishop hotel balcony. On Rishop's hotel balcony, Raju proposed to Puja with a diamond ring and puja accepted it. They plan to marry and go for a honeymoon in this Rishop hotel. We stay there 5 days but our heart says if we stay longer. The next day, we came back to Kalimpong. From there back to Gangtok. From Gangtok we went back to Darjeeling and, from there, back, to home.

---------------------------------- The End

Stunt Man

This story belongs to stun man. His name is Baj. He is 19 years old guy. He hates girls because his mother left him along. He is a movie stun man. His some friends called him Iron man and some friends called him stone man because his body is so strong that if anyone hit his body by hand his hand will be broken. Baj easily passes from fire ring with bike no problem for him and he can easily jump from terrace it not problem for him. He know it stun man life is not an easy one his life also can go. One day his friend's plans go for under water game. They all know swimming so no problem for them. They go by in middle of the sea and stared the game. While going forward they see one whale come toward them. They say Baj to kill that whale. Baj how I kill him with bare hands? They take this gun and kill him. Baj say how I can kill him only his face can see? His friends say try it otherwise he will kill us. Baj fire 6 times but fail to kill him. Suddenly they see one boat come toward their boat they try to catch that boat and they catch it. They get sword from it. Baj take that sword and try to kill that whale. Then they heard someone shouting for help. They say we are in problem now, we can't help now. She says OK. Then Baj kill that whale after 3 time try.

Then they go for help her. They shout where are you? We can help you now but no answer come from her side. After sometime she say just stop the boat and help me to out of here. They pick up her to boat but Baj say to his friends why you all pick up her to the boat? His friends say you just shut up and sit there otherwise we leave you here for few hours. Baj say I will not stay here. Then shut your mouth and sit here. They leave her in a save zone and back to their way. Baj say we need some food now, we are too much hungry. They take the food and plan now go for underwater game. Baj say is already an evening time. His friends say we just not see that. Today time passes too fast. Then they take the way to home. Next morning when he goes for bike stun then he hit one girl side and she fall down. She gets hurts in eyes. They take to the hospital and doctor says she can't see any more. If someone donated her or his eyes then she can again see it. Baj unite say you marry her. Baj say, no I will not marry her but I will try to gets donated eyes for her so she can again see it. After he gets eye then she get surgery and after 10 days eye will open.

After day 10 day her eye will open and doctor say you slowly open your eyes. She opens her eyes and I can see it again. After 7 days she gives realize from hospital. Baj ask doctor for her address and doctor gives it to him. Baj go to her home and ask about her but her father say why you come here? You take my daughter eyes and again she now sees it. It not shoots you. Just go for here and do not come here again but I love her and I want to marry her. Her father say it not be possible. You just get lost from here. Then he goes from there. Her name is Jinni. Baj do not know her name. She meets him outside their home or in park. She also loves him very much because for him she can see it again. She also wants to marry him but her father does not want it. Baj say his mom I want to marry her and his mom say she is good but her dad does not allow you to do that. They are belongs to rice family. Baj say his mom I also earn good money. His mom says you lead a risk full life. Your life can be gone anytime. If you do a secured job then it can be possible. Then Baj and Jinni run out from home and gets married. Then they leave happily married life.

-------------------------------------The End------------------------------------

Office Built On Graveyard

Once upon a time in our city one office built on graveyard, everybody knows it as a haunted office because most of his tower is haunted. Now it becomes an IT hub of our city. The local residents of that place claim that they have seen strange visions in the darkest hours during the night. One day I hear that my friend joint that office, I warm him about that office but he says let see what is happen there. In office he hear that staff are strictly advised not to wander in the Third Floor of the Tower 3 and the floor is shut all most all the time as it is haunted by many ghosts. He also hear that staff working the graveyard shifts in this office have often complained of hearing and seeing things whenever they leave use the lifts or step out of the buildings. He not believes that office some tower is haunted.

He is working in tower 2 second floors. In 4th floor is café area. One day he go to 3th floor there also coffee avail there. When he takes coffee and come toward lift he feels some stand behind him then he move backward to see if anyone there. He saw one girl wear jeans and t-shirt walking from there, he saw from back side but no shoe in legs. He runs towards lift there he saw raw blood, then he just go in to lift come back to 2nd floor and tells to his friends says why you do not believe it. His friend's say why you go to 3nd floor nobody goes there it totally haunted. Then he goes to wash room, there he feel somebody takes deep breathing he scared and run from wash room. When he takes water bottle to drink water he suddenly saw nobody in that room. He come to wrong room, then he try to come out from that room but door is open.

Then he shouts for help suddenly door open he come out of that room. His friend's says why you go to that room nobody goes there. He was so scared that he plans to leave the job. He not goes again to that office to collects his salary also. He leaves that job after one month working.

------------------------------------THE END----------------------------------

Picnic

This story is all about a college picnic at Mandarmani beach. Our principal also goes with us. Her name is Liza. Our Sir and another Madam also go with us. We started at 8:00 AM in the morning. We took a luxury bus. On that bus we have a coffee machine and a video. We take our breakfast by bus with coffee. We enjoy our journey by singing and dancing on the bus. Sir's are also singing with us. We all enjoy it a lot. Suddenly, the bus stopped because of a traffic jam. Outside, there boys are selling sea shell products. Sir called one boy on the bus and all his shell products were sold. See that others also come by bus. Their shell products also sell. Then the bus started again. We reached our guest house. Where we stay for a few hours. The guest house is so beautiful but the caretaker says you all leave here before 7:00 PM. We do not understand why he said that? Our picnic on the beach has started. A cricket match is going to be held for students and Sir. Girls are playing badminton on the other side of the beach. On the other side of the beach, our picnic cooking started. The cricket match is for 5 over. The toss is won by students and they first bat. The game starts now. The first ball wants to hit a sixer but clean bold. Then the second ball wanted to hit four but it caught and out. The student score is now zero for 2 to down. This match is going on. Some girls are playing with sea water. Suddenly, they see someone forcing madam and taking her to the sea water. She shouted for help. Then the girls ran to save her. Then they run out from there when they see girls coming. Then the girls took her to the guest house and said take a rest. We will be outside. She does not understand why someone is trying to kill her? She said, after lunch, late go back.

The cricket match ended with no result because of it. Someone always follows Madam. He tried to kill her and in the guest house room,. He also went inside to kill her with a gun, but the girls saved her again. Then we had lunch and the lunch menu was porn fried rice, mutton kosha, red crab curry, fruit chutney, sweets and ice cream. After lunch, we made our way back home. We all got on the bus and started our journey again. We started singing by dancing on the bus. In the evening, we have coffee with cookies. We enjoy our journey by going back home. Suddenly, someone said stop the bus from outside, but the bus driver did not stop it. Then we went back home. Our

picnic ends here.
-------------------------------------- The End

Contents